WARE

THROUGH TIME

David Perman &
Stephen Jeffery Poulter

AMBERLEY PUBLISHING

The authors would like to thank the Trustees of Ware Museum for allowing us to use images from their postcard and photograph collection for this project, and especially the Curator Elisabeth Barratt for her generous assistance in identifying the images.

First published 2012

Amberley Publishing
The Hill, Stroud
Gloucestershire, GL5 4EP
www.amberley-books.com

Copyright © David Perman & Stephen Jeffery Poulter, 2012

The right of David Perman & Stephen Jeffery Poulter to be identified as the Author of this work has been asserted in accordance with the Copyrights, Designs and Patents Act 1988.

ISBN 978 1 4456 0708 5

British Library Cataloguing in Publication Data.
A catalogue record for this book is available from the British Library.

Typeset in 9.5pt on 12pt Celeste.
Typesetting by Amberley Publishing.
Printed in the UK.

Introduction

The basic road pattern of Ware was established by the year 1191 and has not changed very much since then. I realise that is a bold claim and, of course, it needs some explanation. The fact is that until 1977 Ware was situated on one of the major roads north out of London – in the Middle Ages it was known as the Old North Road and in more modern times the A10. In 1977, the A10 bypass – or Ware bypass – was built on a long viaduct across the Meads, but Ware remained on an important trunk road, now relabelled the A1170. Many older people feel that the traffic has not diminished since the town was bypassed, that in fact it has got worse. The basic reason for this is that all those roads – the Old North Road, the A10 and the A1170 – passed along Ware High Street. That's why I say the basic road pattern has not changed very much.

By comparison with neighbouring towns – I'm thinking of Hertford and Hoddesdon – Ware has not been cut in two by a dual carriageway with all the horrors of pedestrian underpasses. It almost happened; but in the 1960s and '70s the Ware Society fought against the County Surveyor at inquiry after inquiry and delayed things long enough for government thinking to go through a U-turn. 'Urban Motorways' were thrown out and with them went the Ware Inner Relief Road, with all the damage and disruption that would have caused.

Let's go back to 1191 and even earlier, to AD 43 and the Roman conquest. The major road north for the legions was Ermine Street, leading from London to Lincoln, York and Scotland. At Ware, Ermine Street encountered a river that was flowing west to east – our own River Lea – and passed over it by means of a ford. There's no archaeological evidence of a bridge but plenty for a ford. (This ford may later have been called 'Hertford', but that's another story). A small town grew around the ford, catering for the legionaries and other travellers with refreshments, pottery, gifts, etc. Evidence of Ermine Street is found whenever Glaxo's turn the ground to erect a new building on their manufacturing site in Priory Street. When the Saxons arrived (some time later) they moved the road a little way to the east, along the line of what is now Baldock Street.

But the major change happened in the twelfth century. Ware had a new Lady of the Manor and she chose to live in a sumptuous hall within the Benedictine Priory (roughly where St Mary's Church is, and not to be confused with 'The Priory' on the other side of the road). The Lady was Petronilla or Parnel, Countess of Leicester. Working with her son, the Earl of Leicester, and son-in-law, Saer de Quincy, Earl of Winchester, Parnel diverted the road so that it ran parallel with the river to a new bridge, half a mile east of the ford. This was a clever move. It produced a High Street wide enough for markets and fairs; it created 'burgage plots' that could be rented to craftsmen and shopkeepers; it transformed the town from one you passed through to one where you wanted to stay. And it worked – the High Street was soon lined with inns. But it did not pass off without controversy. The bailiff of Hertford Castle put a chain across the new bridge and blocked the ford. Saer de Quincy famously threw the chain into the river and told the bailiff he would follow it if he tried again to interfere.

Ware was a splendid town in the Middle Ages and later. Important people, including royalty, stayed here. The Great Bed of Ware – mentioned by Shakespeare and other writers – was part of this story: all honour to the Ware Museum for persuading the Victoria and Albert Museum to lend them the Great Bed until April 2013. The riverside gazebos were also part of the story. Ware ceased to be a major travellers' town when the road became churned up by the wagons bringing barley to the malting industry. The malting industry gave Ware a new importance, and so did other industries like Allen & Hanburys pharmaceuticals and Wickham's diesel railcars, which were exported throughout the world.

This book is not history of Ware – you can find that in all its fascination and richness in *A New History of Ware: its people and its buildings*, which I wrote in 2010. *Ware Through Time* is a tour of the town, showing how streets, buildings and other scenes have changed since the great age of the postcard, 1902–1914, when it cost a halfpenny to send a postcard and you could be sure your friends would read your message at breakfast the next day. We start the tour in the north-west at Ware Park and follow Park Road into the town. Then we travel down Watton and Wadesmill roads before exploring the town centre and the river, and finally going down Amwell End to the south side. I hope you enjoy this tour of Ware as much as I have in compiling it.

David Perman

The Great Bed of Ware
The Great Bed was first recorded in 1596 by a German Prince who described it as 'so wide, four couples might cosily lie side by side'. In 1610 another German aristocrat saw it in an inn he called The Stag (thought to have been the White Hart at 75 High Street). The Great Bed was later recorded in the George, the Crown and the Bull inns, before being taken to its last Ware home, the old Saracen's Head Inn. In 1869 it left Ware for a show park at Rye House.

Ware Park House

Ware Park became the manor house of Ware in about 1580 when Thomas Fanshawe, the Queen's Remembrancer of the Exchequer, abandoned Place House and began to build a mansion in what had been the medieval game park. Since then there have been many houses on the site. The one pictured above was built in the 1880s but ceased to be the manor house just before the First World War. In 1920 it was purchased by Hertfordshire County Council and became a TB sanatorium. That closed in 1970 when the house was converted into luxury apartments and large detached houses were built in the grounds. The one on the right in the picture below is named 'Fanshawes' and is on the site of the Tudor mansion. *WAEMT 1990.31.80.*

The Avenue, Ware Park

The drive from the town to Ware Park House began in Park Lane (now Park Road), which branched off the Watton Road near the centre of Ware. There was a lodge, built in 1883 , which still there, and after that the drive was flanked by oak trees. Most of the oaks have gone and the footpath, marking the line of the old avenue, is now superseded by a gated road leading to Bardon Farm. The A10 dual carriageway now divides Ware Park from the town and the residents of the former mansion and surrounding houses now look to Bengeo rather than Ware. *WAEMT 1990.31.106.*

Wulfrath Way, Watton Road

In the 1970s, Ware town was allowed to expand into what had been Ware Rural District. This was achieved by building houses right up to the line of the new A10 bypass. The main new developments were the Trapstyles estate, off Park Road, the Old Vicarage estate (*see page 12*) and Wulfrath Way, named after Ware's twin town in Germany. The reason for the sudden drop into Wulfrath Way from Watton Road is that this was once a massive pit for the extraction of sand and brick earth, run by the Skipp and later the Brazier families. William Skipp was a brickmaker, but also founded the town's first cinema and Ware Garage. *WAEMT 1997.15.100.*

Gladstone Road

Gladstone Road is horseshoe shaped with two entrances on to Watton Road. It was built in the 1880s and named after the Liberal Prime Minister, Mr W. E. Gladstone – nearby in Park Road are Palmerston Cottages, named after another Liberal politician. Gladstone Road has always been residential and in this photograph from 1905 Mr Ward and his team pride themselves on 'furniture carefully removed'. The only non-residential building in the road is the British Legion Hall, built after the First World War. *WAEMT 1990.31.138*.

Watton Road

Before the Watton Road roundabout was built in the 1970s, the road made a right-angle junction with Baldock Street, with Percy Moss's cycle shop on the corner. Behind the shop were the Chequers public house, now an estate agent's, and the Star Brewery, now residential. The land at the corner of Watton Road remained a demolition site until the new houses were built in 2000.

Poles Convent

On Ware's northern boundary with Thundridge stood Poles, originally the home of the Hanbury family (of the brewers Truman, Hanbury & Buxton). In 1923 it became a Roman Catholic girls' school, run by the nuns of the Faithful Companions of Jesus (FCJ): their chapel can be seen on the left of this 1950s photograph. The school closed in 1974 and the buildings were converted and enlarged as a luxury golfing hotel, known as Hanbury Manor. Incidentally, the Poles branch of the Hanbury family was only distantly related to the pharmaceutical family of Allen & Hanburys.

Wadesmill Road

The Roman town of Ware lay on Ermine Street, built by the legions as their main route to Lincoln, York and Hadrian's Wall. Wadesmill Road follows the line of Ermine Street, though farther south it was diverted eastwards in Saxon and medieval times. The modern view was taken from the entrance to the Wodson Park sports complex. On the right is Quincey Road, which is a continuation of Wulfrath Way and named after a medieval lord of the manor, Saer de Quincy, Earl of Winchester. *WAEMT 1990.31.122.*

Wadesmill Road, Ware.

Wadesmill Road, Ware

Poles Lane

At the bottom of the hill, as Wadesmill Road veers to the east, there is a junction with Poles Lane, an ancient 'green road' that enabled farm vehicles to bypass the turnpike at Wadesmill. Also on the 1917 postcard is a gate leading to the drive of the 'Old Vicarage' of St Mary's – after which the new houses of the 1970s were named the Old Vicarage estate. *WAEMT 1997.15.5.*

Thunder Hall, Ware.

Thunder Hall

Where Wadesmill Road joins Baldock Street at the corner of The Bourne is a strange building known as Thunder Hall. The name comes from the fact that it was once part of the Manor of Ware Extra and Thundridge. It is a seventeenth- and eighteenth-century house, which in the 1840s was given a Gothic makeover, with a cloister, wagonway entrance and other embellishments. In the 1980s the house was converted into flats and the extensive garden was developed as Thundercourt. *WAEMT 1990.31.20*

Baldock Street, Ware.

Baldock Street

This is the view down Baldock Street from The Bourne in the early years of the twentieth century. On the right is the Hope Malting, one of the largest in Ware, stretching down to Watton Road. On the left is the wall of Haycocks and The Stables. Those two houses are still there, but everything on the right has disappeared to make way for road widening and the construction of the fire station. In the distance is the huge Watton Road roundabout, which is the only part of the Ware Inner Relief Road scheme to be built. *WAEMT 1990.31.21.*

Monkey Row

Construction of the Watton Road roundabout meant the demolition of Monkey Row, including a medieval hall house, seen here when it was Page's bakery. When news of the demolition became known, the house was bought by May Savidge (*right*), who refused to accept compensation and instead announced her intention to move the house to Wells-Next-The-Sea in Norfolk. Despite her efforts, sadly May died before she could finish reassembling and furnishing what she called 'Ware Hall House'. The site is now under the road and entrance to a car park. *WAEMT 1997.15.182.*

Baldock Street

The bottom of Baldock Street, where it joins the High Street, appears much the same as in the photograph of the 1950s. Cruise's bakery on the corner of Priory Street now caters for financial services and there are many more offices in Baldock Street. In the High Street, however, the houses on the left have been replaced by a bus shelter and small garden. The brick wall (*extreme left*) was part of the garden of the Priory Lodge. It is now incorporated into the Ware Museum, which was founded in 1986 and has twice expanded since then. *WAEMT 1997.15.46.*

The Octagon

Under the Poor Law Amendment Act of 1834, the town's poorhouse was abolished and a new Ware Union workhouse built in Collett Road to accommodate those on parish relief not only from Ware, but fourteen other parishes too. It was built in 1837 to the plan of a 'panopticon', with a central control station and wards radiating outwards. After the Second World War, it became part of the NHS and was then known as Western House Infirmary. In the 1970s it was converted to residential use and rechristened the Octagon with the front offices where the Poor Law Guardians had met known as the Old Boardroom. *WAEMT 1990.31.17.*

Crib Street

Crib Street is one of the oldest streets in Ware and the origin of the name is much debated. It was renowned for its abundance of pubs – seen here from the right the Cabin, the Green Dragon and the Albion (further up were the Red Cow, the White Horse and the Prince of Wales). In the 1950s much of Crib Street was blighted by plans for the Ware Inner Relief Road and Central Area Redevelopment. Seen in the modern photograph, the wrought-iron arch was donated by the Ware Society. Behind, on the left, is Church Court, formerly almshouses.

Crib Street

Many of the buildings in this photograph were blighted by the plans for the Relief Road and deteriorated beyond repair. They were then rebuilt as modern buildings in a similar style. In the modern view, the gap beyond the line of parked cars was where the Relief Road would have cut across Crib Street. It is now the entrance to a kindergarten playground. *WAEMT 1997.15.178.*

Musley Hill

New Road and Musley Hill were built in the 1830s as the first expansion of Ware out of the Lea valley on to the surrounding hills. The Rifle Volunteer pub on the corner of Collett Road was originally called the Union Jack. Opposite was a shop owned by the Greenhill family – as they had another shop at the bottom of New Road, this one was known as 'Greenhill far away' (after the hymn 'There is a green hill far away'). Farther up Musley Hill is a row of superior terraced houses known as 'Skippers' Row', intended for the steersmen on the barges taking malt to London. *WAEMT 1990.31.16.*

Musley Lane

Opposite Collett Road is Musley Lane, now blocked off from Musley Hill for safety reasons. Musley Lane with its continuation into Little Widbury Lane was one of the ancient drovers' roads into Ware that avoided the marshy, flood-prone Star Lane. The Standard pub was a drovers' pub. Musley Lane is now a cul-de-sac and has its own younger cul-de-sac, Kiln House Close – named after the large malthouses that were here until about 1964. *WAEMT 1990.31.39.*

New Road

New Road had some of the first detached, middle-class houses in Ware and was also known for the number of its Victorian churches. On the left can be seen the roof of the Catholic Apostolic Church and next door, at No. 50 New Road, was the Zoar Baptist Church – the baptismal pool still exists in the back garden. This postcard dates from before the First World War, when children were paid a penny each to stand absolutely still while the photographer went under a cloth and exposed his glass slide. *WAEMT 1997.15.17.*

Chapel Mews

The Catholic Apostolic Church was founded in 1831 by followers of the Revd Edward Irving, who 'spoke with tongues' (and were sometimes known as 'Irvingites'). They arrived in Ware in the 1840s, first in a chapel in Church Street, and opened this large church in 1857. The denomination was led by twelve apostles and when the last of these died in 1901 he 'sealed' the church, so that no new ordinations took place and no new sermons were written. The last priest in Ware was named Howard and for years his descendants supported the church until its closure in 1952. It then became a furniture store for Fishpools of Waltham Cross. In 1986 it was converted into apartments and became known as Chapel Mews. *WAEMT 1990.31.98.*

Christ Church, Ware

Christ Church

Christ Church was founded in 1858 as the second Anglican parish of the town. The impetus came mainly from Robert Hanbury of Poles, who provided both the land and the funds for the new church, built of Kentish Ragstone (Ware was then in the Diocese of Rochester). Hanbury Close, on the site of the original vicarage, commemorates the founder. Christ Church has a freestanding bell tower but a full peel of bells was decided against so as not to compete with St Mary's. The land behind Christ Church accommodates both the Memorial Hall and the original buildings of Christ Church National Schools (now Christ Church Voluntary Aided JMI). *WAEMT 1997.15.13.*

Christ Church

From its foundation, Christ Church has been an evangelical parish, determined to tackle the major social problems of the town, especially poverty and drink. From 1883 to 1954 it maintained the Mission Hall in Amwell End, one of the poorest areas of Ware, with a lending library, reading and writing rooms, sewing classes, rooms for indoor sports as well as tennis and cricket clubs. When bombs fell in New Road during the Second World War, all of the windows of Christ Church were blown out. *WAEMT 1990.31.78.*

New Road, Ware.

Springs Christian Fellowship

Opposite Christ Church is the chapel, founded by the Wesleyan Methodists in 1839. In 1844 a Methodist minister conducted services in the Town Hall for members of the congregation of St Mary's who objected to High Church ritual. Methodist worship in New Road ceased in 1972 and a few years later Ware's Methodists joined the United Reformed to form the Leaside Church in the High Street. This building is now the Springs Christian Fellowship. The houses on the left were built in the 1840s as model cottages for artisans. *WAEMT 1990.31.113.*

New Road, Ware.

The Red Lion

Maltings lay behind New Road, including the three parallel buildings constructed in 1838 for the making of brown malt. Even before New Road was built this had been the malting yard of the Dickinson family, who lived in what is now East Street. Because of the thirsty work in the malt kilns – and despite the sermons in Christ Church – a number of pubs clustered around the bottom of New Road. On the right is the Red Lion (now a social work centre known as the Warehouse) and opposite were the Plough and the Bell. *WAEMT 1990.31.125.*

New Road, Ware.

Ally Rogers' Stationer's

On the corner of New Road and High Street stood the stationer's and newsagent's owned by A. H. (Ally) Rogers. He was a magistrate, a pillar of the Congregational Church (now Leaside) and was known around the town for his winged collars and spats. Next door was the shop of clock and watchmaker John Ketterer, who came to Ware as a German refugee in 1860. During the First World War his grandson, Constantine Ketterer, was the Quartermaster of the Hertfordshire Regiment in Flanders. Ketterer's is now a restaurant and Rogers' shop is an estate agent's. *WAEMT 1990.31.26.*

Parish Church, Ware, Herts.

The Parish Lock-up

The parish church of St Mary the Virgin has scarcely changed since this postcard of 1908 – but its surroundings have. The building on the right was the police station and lock-up, and next to that was a forge (*see page 35*). On the opposite corner of Church Street, iron railings enclosed what was known as the New Burial Ground. Immediately after the First World War the Boy Scouts hung a memorial on these railings to their lost comrades. And in 1921 the railings were replaced by the tall stone war memorial with the 'Cross of Sacrifice' design by Sir Reginald Bloomfield. *WAEMT 1990.31.24.*

Ware Parish Church

The Parish Church

When this postcard was issued in 1910, the interior of St Mary's was much as it had been after the two Victorian restorations in 1849 and 1880. It was a dark building, still lit by gas supplied by the Ware Gas, Light & Coke Company and on the stone walls were the fading texts and images that had so delighted Victorian worshippers. The contrast with St Mary's today is striking. The interior was painted white in the 1960s and a few years later a wooden altar was placed in the nave, so that the priest would face the congregation during celebration of the Eucharist. *WAEMT 1992.7.56.*

c 1900

The Parish Church

Other changes at St Mary's took place outside. In the 1970s, after a careful recording of the names and location of each burial, the gravestones were placed against the walls of the churchyard. An extension, now known as St Mary's Hall, was built in the 1980s with funds received for the sale of the Parish Clerk's Field when the A10 bypass was being constructed. The hall includes a large meeting room, a smaller children's room, choir vestry, toilets and kitchen. But the Vicar's Vestry, seen left, remains in use. *WAEMT 1997.15.7.*

Church Street

This part of Church Street was once known as Steeple End. It was a cul-de-sac ending in the church and the old St Mary's Vicarage. When the vicarage was demolished and its garden made into the new burial ground, the road went through to the High Street. These cottages were demolished in the 1970s to make way for Church Row Mews (*below centre*). The building on the right was the Vicar's Room, part of the St Mary's National Schools. The Vicar's Room is now offices and the school is a doctors' surgery. *WAEMT 1997.15.176.*

Church Street

The tall building was used by Ware's fire brigade for its long 'escape' ladder. The Ware brigade was created by the Local Board of Health (forerunner of Ware Urban District Council) and soon replaced the private fire brigades operated by insurance companies. In 1907 the council purchased a steam-driven engine to replace hand pumps, but it was horse-drawn. The brigade did not have an efficient motorised engine until 1930, when a 60 hp Merryweather engine was purchased. The area is now a car park for nearby offices. *WAEMT 1997.15.173.*

Church Street

This part of Church Street was once known as French Horn Lane, named after the former pub nearer the High Street. Three of the cottages on the right of the photograph survive; the others have been demolished to make way for the entrance to the Tesco car park (in the former builders' yard of F. Hitch & Co. Ltd) and the small industrial estate known as Hitches Yard. *WAEMT 1997.15.175*.

Town Forge

For many years, the town forge occupied the corner of Church Street and the High Street. In later years, the forge was run by G. A. Yorke & Son, who moved across to Priory Street in what is now Yorke Mews. The site then became a memorial garden. In 1999 – to commemorate the millennium and the end of the malting industry in Ware after 600 years – the statue known as *The Maltmaker* was unveiled in the memorial garden. It was designed by Jill Tweed and funded by the Stanstead Abbots maltsters French & Jupp, as well as private donors. *WAEMT 1997.15.227.*

Churchgate House

Churchgate House in West Street is a fascinating amalgam of medieval houses. There are at least three crown-post roofs and many other timber-framed features, including a dragon post where the jetties meet. The houses were brought together to form a courtyard in the seventeenth century and were at one time an inn, the Eagle and Child. In the nineteenth century, it was the bakery of Jaggs & Edwards, where many of the townspeople had their Sunday lunch baked – especially at Christmas. The building was restored in 1999 and is now Jacoby's restaurant. *WAEMT 1997.15.192.*

West Street

West Street was at one time the original north side of the High Street and known as Land Row. The buildings on its south side, known as Middle Row, were former market stalls that became permanent. The north side was also lined with cottages until the 1960s when they were demolished to make way for a car park and the town's telephone exchange. In 1999, the car park was paved with brick and designated for use by the Tuesday market. Restaurants and flats were built on the square's northern edge, and it was given the name Tudor Square after the Tudor Free Grammar School, which stood here until about 1883. *WAEMT 1997.15.177.*

The Priory, Ware.

The Priory

This is one of Ware's most important buildings, but its name is incorrect. The medieval Priory of Ware was elsewhere and this building was a Franciscan Friary – parts of the friars' cloister can be seen on the left. After Henry VIII's dissolution of religious houses, it became a private residence and remained so until 1913, when it was then bought by Mrs A. E. Croft, only child of Ware's millionaire maltster Henry Page. She allowed it to be used as a convalescent hospital during the First World War and in 1920 gave it to the town on a 999-year lease. It is now the offices of Ware Town Council, which bought the freehold and carried out an extensive restoration in 1993/94. *WAEMT 1990.31.110.*

Ware Priory, South Front

The Priory

The rear of the Priory shows the country manor house that it was before 1913. As well as the lawns and the large greenhouse (now a dining facility), there is a first-floor drawing room with a turret window and the Garden Room, erected in the 1890 as a billiards room. The estate includes extensive gardens on the banks of the River Lea, an island, a children's playground and a modern conference centre named Fletcher's Lea after a former town clerk. *WAEMT 1997.15.19.*

The Lido

The lido in Priory Street was built on the Priory orchard in 1934 by the council's own labourers, using hardcore from recently demolished 'slum' dwellings. It was designed by the Ware Council surveyor, Robert Grantham, and widely admired by other councils. It is now one of the few heated outdoor pools in Hertfordshire, if not the only one. It is still owned by Ware Town Council, assisted by the Friends of Ware Lido. *WAEMT 1999.16.20.*

High St. Ware.

High Street

In the Tudor period the south side of the High Street was known as Water Row and had up to twenty-six large inns. Their wagonways can still be seen beneath what appear to be eighteenth- and nineteenth-century shops and houses, though many are in fact timber framed. The Tap Bar (formerly the Brewery Tap) is the last of these licensed houses in Water Row. It was once the Horseshoe Inn, whose landlord was the postmaster in Tudor times. Next door were the offices of Henry Page & Co., Ware's largest malting firm, with their malthouses behind. When these were demolished in the 1960s the land was used as the library car park. *WAEMT 1990.31.76.*

High Street

The north side of the High Street was a mixture of low, timber-framed buildings – medieval market stalls that had become permanent – and tall, Victorian intrusions. The building with a turret was a pub: originally the Clarendon then renamed the Vine and latterly the Wine Lodge. Next door was a shop owned by a Mr Parrett, who jumped from the first-floor window when it burned down. The Wine Lodge has now closed down and the gap next door leads through to Tudor Square. *WAEMT 1990.31.50.*

R. W. Harradence

The marks on this 1910 postcard indicate the extent of Harradence's department store. It was founded in 1775 by Robert Harradence as a haberdasher's, and over the next two centuries it expanded westwards, adding dressmaking, millinery, gents' outfits, boots and shoes, carpets, curtains and china to its stock. It was the only part of the High Street where the back land did not become a malting yard – in consequence it was known as the 'secret garden'. Harradence's closed in 1971, just short of 200 years, and the land behind was developed as Burgage Court. *WAEMT 1990.31.84.*

Gilpin House

No. 84 High Street gained the name Gilpin House when it was used as an illustration to William Cowper's poem about John Gilpin's unintended ride to Ware. In fact, it is part of an early Tudor building, added to in the seventeenth century when fireplaces and ceilings were decorated with plasterwork. Some say it was built by Henry VII for his mother, Margaret Countess of Richmond, but there is no evidence for that. This postcard of 1916 shows it as the Blue Boot Stores. It has recently been restored and is now a ladies' hairdresser's. *WAEMT 1990.31.5.*

The Town Hall

This was one of two buildings that claimed to be the Town Hall – the other was in Rankin Square. In fact, it was built by public subscription in 1827 as a replacement for the Tudor Market House, which was falling down, and intended to attract the corn dealers away from Hertford Market. But it never worked and instead it became a butcher's shop for the Stallabrass family. Upstairs was a newspaper reading room, which was used later for boxing tournaments. The building is now an estate agent's. *WAEMT 1990.31.9.*

Market Place

In the early Middle Ages markets extended along the whole High Street, but by 1920 they were confined to the area outside the Town Hall or Cornmarket. This display of old limousines and taxis was brought together by Mr A. D. Skipp, who owned the Ware Garage at 66 High Street. Ware Garage expanded into Church Street before moving to the Ware Road, Hertford, in the 1990s when Boots the Chemist took over the building. *WAEMT 1997.15.65.*

Falcon Ironworks

This building at Nos 49–51 High Street, was the Bear Inn in Tudor times; the deeds from this time say it was 'anciently called the Falcon'. In the nineteenth century it became the Falcon Foundry & Ironworks, owned by an innovative engineer named Charles Wells. His specialities were wire floors for the kilns of malthouses and the wrought-iron tie-plates that held the floors in place. He also designed and produced many of the cowls to top the malt kilns. When he died in 1860, the company was taken over by A. J. Goodfellow. The building is now a travel agent and stationery/printing works.

Gideon Talbot

Next to the Falcon Ironworks was Gideon Talbot's motor and cycle business – with a petrol pump whose arm swung into the High Street. This building and its neighbour were demolished in the 1970s to make way for a link to a service road (parallel with the river) that was never built. That plan accounts for the wide arch next to Greggs bakery.

The Flower de Luce

Also demolished to make way for the service road was this large seventeenth-century building, originally an inn named the Flower de Luce (Fleur de Lys). In the nineteenth century it became the 'Ware Library' of the printer, George Price, later taken over by Simson Pimm and Jennings & Bewley. In the 1970s it became Tesco Home and Wear and more recently Peacocks. *WAEMT 1992.7.65.*

The French Horn

Opposite was the French Horn Inn, which had its own theatre for repertory companies in the nineteenth century. The road – originally called Dead Lane – was then known as French Horn Lane and is now Church Street. The French Horn became residential in the 1980s – the rooms above Ware Card Centre are part of that development. *WAEMT 1990.31.65.*

The George Inn

No. 31 High Street (along with what are now Lloyds TSB and Barclays banks) was part of the George Inn. It was frequented by fishermen and is mentioned in Isaak Walton's *Compleat Angler*. In the early twentieth century it was the shop of a member of the large Page family, who were also corn and coal merchants. It is now a hairdresser's. The wagonway leads to George Walk. *WAEMT 1997.15.156.*

Charles Forbes

At one time there were many drapers' shops in Ware, for men's, women's and children's wear. At No. 54 was the shop of Charles Forbes, general draper. The shop is photographed here in 1921 with the three assistants – the Misses Figg, Head and Knights. After years of divided ownership, the building is now a combined jewellery and gift shop.

East Street

East Street, like West Street (see page 37), once formed the northern side of the High Street before the buildings of Middle Row intervened. On the corner was this shop, which in the 1950s was the Ware Hardware Stores, owned by Gerald Sayer, who later moved it into East Street. This shop then became Donoghue's fishmonger's and is now the Isobel Hospice charity shop. East Street is now pedestrianised. *WAEMT 1997.15.45.*

Cooper's Cigar Stores

In the days when smoking was big business, George Cooper had a tobacco and cigar stores at No. 34 High Street, with a warehouse in the basement and a wholesale business behind in East Street (now the Dolphin House Surgery). No. 34 is now a Thai restaurant with the eating area in the basement.

High Street

This part of the High Street – seen from the bottom of New Road – is not now very different from this 1910 postcard. There is still a jeweller's on the left (then Ketterer's, now Wren's) but the Bay Horse pub on the right has now become part of the adjoining pub, then called the Bell and now the Vine. *WAEMT 1990.31.90.*

The Saracen's Head Inn

The big change in this part of the High Street is the loss of the Saracen's Head Inn, demolished in 1957 for road widening. The inn, seen above in a 1908 photograph, was one of the oldest in Ware, dating from the thirteenth century and the last home in the town of the Great Bed. The wagonway next to the inn led to a yard where markets and auctions were held and to an assembly hall with a clock and the inscription *Tempus Fugit* (time flies). The modern shops were originally owned by McMullens the brewery. *WAEMT 1997.15.160.*

Bridgefoot

In August 1914, D Company of the 1st Hertfordshire Volunteer Regiment marched around the tight corner of Bridgefoot on their way to training and distinguished service in the trenches of the First World War. They were led by Lieut. Colonel Henry Page Croft, on horseback. The modern Bridgefoot lacks the Barge Inn on the right and the old buildings on the left, but the buildings in the centre of the photograph survive. *WAEMT 1997.15.66.*

Bridgefoot

No. 12 High Street was built in the early eighteenth century for a wealthy Quaker maltster. In the early twentieth century it became a department store of the Enfield Highway Co-operative Society, which had a milk depot and bakery next door – the bakery's mosaic sign is still there in Star Street. The building was restored in the 1990s with the bonus of a pedestrian way into the Kibes Lane car park.

Vicarage Road

Vicarage Road was created in the early years of the twentieth century as an extension of King Edward's Road. It never contained a vicarage but was visible from the vicarage of Christ Church in New Road. When it was proposed to build a public house on the corner of King Edward's Road and Bowling Road, the Revd. Alfred Oates vetoed the plan because it would have been visible from the vicarage windows – instead the building became a shop and is now a house. *WAEMT 1990.31.46.*

Kibes Lane

Kibes Lane – running from New Road to Bowling Road – was one of the poorest and most overcrowded streets in Ware. The name is said to be derived from 'kipes' – osier baskets for catching fish (osiers or rushes were common in this part of Ware). The overcrowded houses were demolished in the 1930s slum clearance and the licences of two pubs (the Old Harrow and Jolly Bargeman) transferred to the King George estate. Kibes Lane is now car parks.

Ware Gasworks

The gasworks at the corner of Bowling Road and Star Street originally produced gas from coal for the Ware Gas, Light & Coke Co. It became redundant when natural gas was discovered in the North Sea. Polluted soil had to be removed before the site could be redeveloped. The apartments there are named Bowsher Court, after Charles Bowsher, a former Town Mayor.

Star Street

Star Street was originally a very narrow lane, liable to flooding from the old River Lea. It was widened in the 1920s when the North Metropolitan Electric Power Supply Co. built an office block on the site of the Barge Inn and Bridge Brewery. North Met House later became known as Bridge House and is now the Navigator pub.

Star Street

Because of its proximity to the river and its wharves, Star Street had large malthouses on both sides of the road. On the north side these buildings, which have two different types of kiln cowls, were demolished in the early 1970s when the UK malting business was becoming concentrated into three or four large companies. The malthouses were replaced by a warehouse and that in turn was replaced by housing. *WAEMT 1997.15.249.*

Star Street

Other malthouses – like these Omega Maltings on the south side of Star Street – were refurbished as riverside apartment blocks. In the background, on the other side of the river, is the silo of the Frenlite flour mill, owned by J. W. French & Co. Ltd. *WAEMT 1997.15.68.*

Frenlite Mill

The Frenlite mill, which specialised in self-raising flour, was built beside a cut in the River Lea that at one time gave access to a large barge basin. J. W. French rebuilt it in 1897 and then moved his flour milling from Priory Street, making this a steam-driven mill. The mill closed in the 1980s, the cut was filled in and the old building was incorporated in a large block of apartments with access in Station Road.

Wickham's

Opposite the mill on Viaduct Road was the No.1 Works of D. Wickham & Co., engineers and railcar manufacturers. Even before Wickham's closed its Crane Mead premises in 1991, No. 1 Works had closed and been sold for development. Wickham's Wharf was designed by Rock Townsend, the architects for the Vivat Ware project – its best aspect is from the river. *WAEMT 1997.15.80.*

Ware Park Mill

Ware Park Mill was an overshot mill, with the water coming from the hill above via a leat from the River Rib. It was built in 1721 by James Fordham who also had a malting on the site. The mill has now gone but the outflow of the leat into the River Lea survives. *WAEMT 1990.31.32.*

The White House

The White House was a tearoom and boat hiring centre on the River Lea, between Ware and Hertford. It was a favourite spot for walkers who had gone out 'over the Park' and returned 'under the Park' – Ware Park. The site is now under the huge viaduct, which since 1977 has carried the A10 Ware bypass over the Meads. *WAEMT 1990.31.12.*

The Lock, Ware

Ware Lock

The first lock at Ware was built in the late seventeenth century to allow barges from Hertford to join the navigable river below the natural weirs. It was rebuilt in 1831 by William Chadwell Mylne with a lock-keeper's house (as above). In 1977, the Thames Water Authority built a large weir and siphon system to the south of the lock, as part of the River Lee Flood Relief Channel. *WAEMT 1997.31.35.*

Allen & Hanburys' Mills

The oldest mill in Ware was in Priory Street (formerly Mill Lane). It was purchased by Allen & Hanburys in 1898, when they moved their dried milk production from Bethnal Green. 'Allenburys' later developed the land beside the millstream. It is now the site of Glaxo Global Manufacturing & Supply – part of GlaxoSmithKline, which has a large pharmaceutical research facility in Park Road. *WAEMT 1990.31.8.*

Ware, River Lea.

Riverside Gazebos

The riverside gazebos (formerly known as 'Dutch summerhouses') began to appear in the late seventeenth century, so that guests at the inns could escape the noise and dirt of the High Street. The first were built in the reign of William of Orange, probably in imitation of the summerhouses on the canals of the Netherlands. Most are constructed of timber and have been renewed over the centuries. Many were restored in the 1980s as part of a Ware Society initiative. *WAEMT 1997.31.29.*

Riverside Gazebos

The first gazebo to be restored in 1984 was this two-storey brick-and-timber building. The photograph from the 1930s shows two members of the Harradence family (*see page 43*) being punted across the river. Punting is no longer possible since the deep dredging in 1977 for the Flood Relief Channel. *WAEMT 1995.16.18.*

Riverside Gazebos

At one time there were twenty-six summerhouses between the Priory and the road bridge – there are still eight, the largest group anywhere in England. They fell into disrepair after the Second World War, when there were plans for a service road between the High Street and the river and the private owners were unwilling to invest in their restoration. But the Ware Society raised £6,000 and thus unlocked restoration funds from the government and local councils. *WAEMT 1997.15.25.*

Ware Bridge
In the 1950s the timber merchants Glickstein's moved its stock by barge to Ware. Here the horse-drawn barge *Windsor* is seen coming under the bridge with the horse and horseman Harry Butcher on the right. The maltings by the bridge were demolished along with the old Saracen's Head Inn for road widening. The new Saracen's Head was then built on the riverside. *WAEMT 1997.15.138.*

Ware Bridge
The riverside above Ware Bridge had both working malthouses and gazebos for leisure, but most of the wharves were below the bridge. These barges were probably on their way to Hertford. Nowadays, the only river craft are narrowboats and the Lea at Ware is a leisure river. *WAEMT 1997.15.23.*

Ware Bridge

Once upon a time, any vehicle passing over Ware Bridge had to pay a toll. In the Middle Ages the tolls went to the bailiff of Hertford Castle, but were later granted by King Charles I to the Earl of Salisbury. Ware Urban District Council bought back the tolls from the Marquess of Salisbury in 1911. *WAEMT 1996.1.6.*

THE RIVER AT WARE.

Corn Stores

Below the bridge were the main wharves from which malt was shipped to the London brewers. On the right are the seventeenth-century corn stores, used by Cromwell's cavalry in 1647. Towering above is a grain dryer, which almost burned down in the 1960s – the bottom floor survives as a furniture warehouse, just beyond the Ware Bathroom Centre in the modern photograph. *WAEMT 1997.15.32.*

908 River Lea and Maltings, Ware

Grain Dryer

Another view of the grain dryer, seen from beside the bridge on this postcard of 1908. Some of the riverside maltings in the middle distance survive as housing. The main difference is what was once a commercial river is now a river of leisure. *WAEMT 1990.31.14.*

Albany's Wharf

The main barge operator was Albany's, whose wharf was in Star Street. In the 1930s it was taken over by the Thames Steam Tug & Lighterage Co., which introduced steel barges with names beginning with T, V or W. In the distance is the lock-keeper's cottage of the half-lock where the old river leaves the Lee Navigation. Locally it was known as Willy Lott's Cottage, after the John Constable painting. *WAEMT 1997.15.145.*

Amwell End

Amwell End (so called because it was once in Great Amwell parish) was part of the Old North Road to London and formed part of the Cheshunt turnpike. Following the dispute over the railway crossing (see page 88), the turnpike was diverted along Viaduct Road. Amwell End was the poorest area of the Victorian town, housing the bargees and the loadsmen who loaded the barges with malt. They lived in some of the most crowded and insanitary houses in Ware, crammed into ten yards. A public health report of 1849 stated that in Dickenson's Yard there were twenty-eight houses but only two privies over an open cesspool – the privies were replaced by water closets (WCs) only after a piped water supply was provided. The result of such insanitary conditions was that diseases like cholera and typhus were endemic and Ware scored as badly as industrial Lancashire for infant mortality. *WAEMT 1990.31.44.*

Chapel Yard

The biggest of the yards was Chapel Yard. Its entrance was an archway between two shops. The houses were grouped around a cobbled courtyard and had no sanitation or washing facilities inside – the photograph on the right was taken in 1933 when there was still no internal plumbing and a hand-operated wringer was used to squeeze the water out of the family's washing. Communal WCs were installed as a result of the 1849 public health report and in the 1930s a start was made on demolishing the yards. However, they did not finall disappear from Amwell End until the early 1970s. *WAEMT 1997.15.215; WAEMT 1997.15.211.*

Chapel Yard

Demolition of Chapel Yard. Farther down is the Mission Hall, run by Christ Church with clubs, sports and reading rooms for the inhabitants of the yards. That too was demolished in the 1970s. Beyond it was the Astoria Cinema, converted first into a shopping arcade called Beckett's Walk and then into a nightclub. *WAEMT 1997.15.191.*

Clark's the Butchers

One of the oldest shops in Amwell End was Clark's the butchers, situated between Old Horn Court and Cow Yard. The reason for the names is that the Clark family had an abattoir behind their shop. When it became a kebab house in the 1970s the shopfront was changed.

Spread Eagle

Two doors away is the Spread Eagle pub. The original Spread Eagle was further south, in the path of the railway, so the Northern & Eastern Railway Company built the new pub here. Leatherland's, next door, was once the Amwell End post office and is now a cycle shop. *WAEMT 1990.31.34.*

Monumental Mason

On the corner of Station Road was the workshop and showroom of Mr Smith, monumental and general mason. He did a roaring trade in the days when almost everyone was buried in the cemetery at the top of Watton Road and cremations were rare. The yard is now a car showroom.

Amwell End

The east side of Amwell End, on the right in this 1905 postcard, looks much the same as it does today. In the centre of the row is the Drill Hall, built in 1899 on the site of Dickenson's Yard for D Company of the Hertfordshire Volunteers. It is now owned by East Hertfordshire Council but run as a community facility by the Ware Drill Hall Association. *WAEMT 1990.31.116b.*

Victoria Malting

Behind Amwell End was the Victoria Malting, built in 1907 by Henry Page & Co. and in its time the largest malting in Britain. The barley and malt were moved around by hydraulic pumps and the whole process was run on an industrial scale. It ceased operating in the 1960s and was used for storage until 1988 when it burned down. There is now the Farecla factory on the site. *WAEMT 1990.31.116b.*

Level Crossing, Amwell End, Ware

Ware Crossing

Amwell End was part of the Cheshunt Turnpike. On a Saturday night in October 1843 when the railway company put rails across the turnpike road, there was an almighty row and intense legal argument. The upshot was that the railway company was forced to divert the turnpike along the new Viaduct Road. The branch line was originally single track: when it was doubled a few years later no attempt was made to put a second line across Amwell End. *WAEMT 1997.15.267.*

Ware Station

Ware station in 1910, when carriages and carts from the inns met the trains. The station was threatened with demolition and replacement by a glass box, but a campaign led by the Ware Society saved it. However, it was later changed and 'upgraded'. *WAEMT 1990.31.49.*

Ware Station

A train from Liverpool Street entering Ware station in 1957. The tracks on the right were goods sidings, mainly used for the coal wagons of William Page & Son. The branch line from Broxbourne to Hertford East was electrified in 1960. *WAEMT 1997.15.117.*

Ware from 'Scotts' Hill.

Myddleton Road

The south side of Ware began to be developed after the death of Mrs Hooper, daughter of the poet and grotto-builder John Scott, and the sale of Amwell House and its gardens for development. This photograph claims to be Scott's Hill but is in fact Myddleton Road, which had a view across the Meads to St Mary's Church. The road was named after Sir Humphrey Myddelton, creator of the New River, but the local council misspelled his name. *WAEMT 1992.7.63.*

Amwell House

In 1906, Amwell House – which had been rebuilt and enlarged by John Scott – became the Ware Grammar School for Girls. The assembly hall and classrooms can be seen on the right. The grammar school moved to Presdales House in Hoe Lane in the 1960s and Amwell House was then threatened with demolition so that the road to Hertford could be widened. The building was saved, but with the two protruding wings cut back, and it became part of Ware College (now Hertford Regional College).

Ware Grammar School for Girls.

Amwell House

The photograph of 1920 shows the garden behind the house being used for games. The classrooms are on the left. The garden is now an enclosed area between the modern lecture blocks of the college. The buildings on the left are part of the college's new Inspires Hair and Beauty Salons. *WAEMT 1990.31.127.*

London Road Amwell near Ware.

The Johnny Gilpin Pub

London Road in 1910 with the Johnny Gilpin pub at the corner of what was then Mount Street. The street later became Gilpin Road and the pub was transferred farther to the west. John Gilpin was the hero of the poem by William Cowper, in which a London merchant is taken to Ware against his will by a runaway horse. *WAEMT 1990.31.82.*

London Road, Ware, showing the John Gilpin.

The New River

This postcard of 1911 shows London Road with the New River flowing beside it. The New River was constructed in 1613 to take drinking water into London, and still does so. But it had to skirt around an old house that Sir Hugh Myddelton failed to buy. That is the building in the distance, known as the Red House. *WAEMT 1990.31.66.*

The Red House, London Rd, Ware.
Large & Small Parties Catered for, Tea-Gardens,
Ground for Sports.   H.O. Webster (Proprietor)

The Red House

The original Red House was demolished long ago but the kink in the New River remains. Across the road, there was the Red House tearoom and gardens, popular with walkers and cyclists. The site later became the Red House Garage, but no longer sells petrol, offering car washes instead. *WAEMT 1990.31.88.*